IMAGES OF ENGLAND

BLACKPOOL

AERIAL VIEW OF BLACKPOOL.

IMAGES OF ENGLAND

BLACKPOOL

DAVE THOMPSON

This book is dedicated to Doreen & Harry.

Frontispiece: Aerial view of Blackpool in the 1930s when seven million people a year were flocking to the town – almost double the number of people visiting the resort twenty years earlier. What had started as a centre for cotton workers widened its appeal to become Britain's best-known and best-loved tourist resort.

First published in 2007 by Tempus Publishing

Reprinted in 2010 by
The History Press
The Mill, Brimscombe Port,
Stroud, Gloucestershire, GL5 2QG
www.thehistorypress.co.uk

British Library Cataloguing in Publication Data.
A catalogue record for this book is available from the British Library.

ISBN 978 0 7524 4494 9

Typesetting and origination by Tempus Publishing
Printed and bound in Great Britain

Contents

Acknowledgements

I would like to record my appreciation of the many individuals and organisations who generously provided photographs, shared memories or freely parted with factual material for use in this book. I am grateful to Newton Ashley, Dudley Caton, Serena Daroubakhsh, Frank Dean, Dan Donson, Andrew Gladwell, Hubert Greaves, Leisure Parcs, Ted Lightbown, Robert Mack, Manchester Locomotive Society, Bob Miller, Omnicolour, Dave Ramsbottom, Lesley Ramsbottom (Manchester), Helen Sage, Harry Thompson, The Jess Yates Estate, and the staff of Blackpool Central Library for their goodwill and support.

I am indebted to George Teare at Warkworth New Zealand for his enduring effort in checking my manuscripts.

Introduction: Memories of Blackpool

Universally known throughout the world, few towns conjure up such stirring impressions as Blackpool. Cheerfully unpretentious and brash with all the trimmings one would expect of a traditional seaside resort, Blackpool remains the iconic resort town, but there is more to its richly coloured history than you might think.

The town takes its name from a pool which passed to the sea through peaty soils, giving rise to dark, discoloured waters and ultimately, in the seventeenth century, to the name of 'Blacke-poole'. For centuries it consisted of no more than a few scattered fishermen's dwellings and farmsteads on the coastal dunes and so Blackpool may have remained but for the emerging medicinal fashion of sea bathing and drinking seawater, popularised initially by the wealthy and genteel.

In 1788 the writer William Hutton of Birmingham visited Blackpool and described the area at that time as comprising about fifty houses and lodgings, scattered across a mile of seafront. Hutton wrote, 'in some of these are lodged the inferior class, whose sole motive for visiting this airy region is health.' He describes how the rich rode in carriages or on horseback over the sands whilst poorer visitors found 'equal pleasure in using their feet.'

The expansion and growth of the blossoming resort may well have continued to take a slow course but for an unexpected boost in 1840 when the Preston & Wyre Railway was built to Poulton, putting Blackpool within spitting distance for rail passengers. Within the year the town experienced record business, providing the impetus for a branch line to be constructed to Blackpool itself in 1846. The railway age initially brought mainly the moneyed middle classes but later, from about the 1870s, working-class families from the smoke-ridden industrial heartlands started coming in their droves, feeding an almost incessant thirst for boarding houses, hotels and entertainment.

The second half of the nineteenth century was undoubtedly the most formative era in Blackpool's history and the most significant attractions for visitors were developed at this time. The first pier was constructed in 1863, followed some years later by those three grand palaces of amusement, the Winter Gardens, Alhambra and Blackpool Tower. By the end of the century, four million patrons a year were basking in the enjoyment that Blackpool offered. The town was granted its charter to form the Borough in 1876, laying the municipal foundations for building strong local communities. The town's population had almost doubled over the previous decade and new churches, schools and recreational facilities were built to accommodate the expanding town. Social and sporting groups flourished; amongst these was Blackpool Football Club. From scant beginnings in 1887, the club emerged as one of the top-flight teams of the 1930s and beyond, who in 1953 were to win one of the most famous ever FA Cup finals.

Bold Blackpool has always been at the forefront of pioneering adventure. In 1879 it became the first town to introduce the new-fangled idea of street lighting and was also the first place in England to have an electric tramway – a tradition that is still going strong in Blackpool, decades after most other towns and cities have removed their trams. Before anyone had seriously considered the importance of flight, the first aviators were displaying their airborne skills in Blackpool in 1909 at one of the first ever air shows.

In the roaring twenties, visitors were keen to step out of doors. The decade heralded the construction of Stanley Park, the open-air baths and, after a brief flirtation with carnivals, the re-emergence of the Illuminations. Barring the wartime blackout that lasted until 1949, this tradition has developed into another Blackpool institution. Jayne Mansfield, Gracie Fields and even three-time Grand National winner, Red Rum, have had the distinction of switching on the famous lights.

From 1939 Blackpool made a huge contribution to the war effort and was arguably a beneficiary with all accommodation now full to bursting. It served as an evacuation centre for 90,000 people, mostly children, and then, on the fall of Dunkirk, 70,000 troops were billeted here. During the war 769,673 RAF recruits received initial training at Blackpool and in the Vickers-Armstrong's factory at Squires Gate almost 10,000 people helped with the manufacture of warplanes. Remarkably, only forty-five bombs and thirty incendiaries fell on the town.

The 1950s and '60s witnessed the era of car-driving trippers and, with some demolition and rebuilding works, Blackpool reaffirmed itself as the brashest and best resort of them all, even though some resorts were in meltdown as tourists were now discovering the excitement of holidays to foreign shores. In 1963 the standard rate for full board was still only £1 per day and 4,500 hotels and guesthouses were more than happy to take your money.

Captured throughout this book are cherished resort scenes, landmark buildings, old modes of transport and glimpses of some of the key moments in Blackpool's past. Some pictures were chosen to reveal how the town looked to past generations; others simply to stir the mind's eye. I hope you enjoy this impression of Blackpool.

Dave Thompson

one

A Stroll Along
the Prom

An impression of 'Olde Blackpool' that is reputed to be from 1750, though the buildings here would suggest a later date. The first bathers probably began arriving from about this time to enjoy the new-fangled craze of sea bathing.

An early engraved print of Fox Hall, earliest of the well-known buildings to have been built on the seafront. In the eighteenth century Fox Hall was the hunting lodge of the Tyldesley family of Myerscough but later became a hotel.

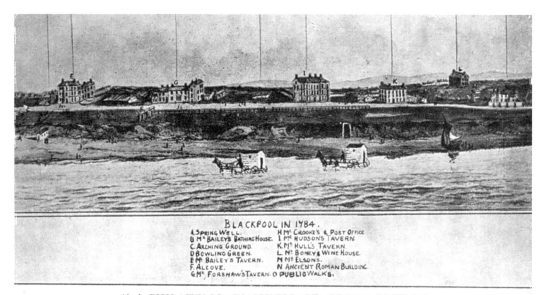

BLACKPOOL IN 1784.

A. Spring Well.
B. Mr Bailey's Bathing House.
C. Arching Ground.
D. Bowling Green.
E. Mr Bailey's Tavern.
F. Alcove.
G. Mr Forshaw's Tavern.
H. Mr Crooke's & Post Office.
I. Mr Hudson's Tavern.
K. Mr Hull's Tavern.
L. Mr Boney's Wine House.
M. Mr Elson's.
N. Ancient Roman Building.
O. Public Walks.

43rd PHILATELIC CONGRESS OF GREAT BRITAIN
BLACKPOOL, 6th—9th JUNE, 1961

This image pinpoints how Blackpool appeared in 1784. Various taverns are shown as well as the post office of Mr George Cook. The postmaster-cum-businessman also established a library and general store reputed to have sold everything from gin to gunpowder. Passenger coaches from Manchester had already been established by this time and the Baylies Hotel (now the Metropole Hotel) was advertising for patrons in the *Manchester Mercury*.

This engraving from the late 1830s shows the view looking north from the Royal Hotel. The promenade was completed in 1837 and from this time, lofty hotels began to spread along its length and across the seafront.

Blackpool sands as they appeared in 1845. The following year Blackpool gained its first railway station, and from that time an ever-increasing number of visitors began to arrive. To the left of this image the Metropole Hotel can be seen in the distance.

These wheeled contraptions are 'bathing machines' and they were hired to help spare the blushes of bathers. Inside the wheeled huts, customers changed into beach attire before horses pulled the hut to the water's edge. Bells were rung several times a day to warn men that women were entering the sea, at which point they were expected to leave or risk fines. The large building standing on the seafront in this image from 1876 is the Metropole Hotel.

Above: The promenade has undergone many sea defence schemes and improvements over the past century and a half. It was widened to 100ft between 1900 and 1905 and further works began again between 1909 and 1911 to cater for the ever-expanding number of visitors. To the left of this image are some of the promenade works underway in 1910.

Below: A view along the stylish promenade in 1911. Hundreds of visitors appear to be enjoying the atmosphere of the new prom.

Linked arm in arm, these promenade strollers are pictured by the South Shore in 1910. Seven miles of promenade are thronged with gaily-dressed visitors, appreciative of the many forms of entertainment found in the vicinity of Blackpool's three piers. To the left of this picture is the South Pier.

Sand-pumping trails are pictured taking place on the promenade, 1905.

A typical picture postcard view of Princess Parade, *c.* 1912. Despite the difficulty of photographing busy promenades – with cumbersome cameras and curious onlookers who moved and spoilt the pictures – Blackpool stationers were able to produce hundreds of different images, sending scenes of Blackpool to all corners of Britain and the Empire.

A 1917 view of the 400-yard long Princess Parade. Standing prominently at one end of the parade is the Metropole Hotel, one of the oldest and best-known hotels in Blackpool. The hotel has had many names in the past and has a colourful history dating back to around 1776. For a time the Metropole was owned by Butlins – complete with its own resident redcoats.

Princess Parade Blackpool.

Above: The construction of Blackpool Tower is well underway in this picture from 1892. The building works required the use of 2,500 tons of steel and more than five million bricks. The tower opened in 1894 and gave the promenade its most striking emblem.

Right: It boasted being the 'wonderland of the world' and not surprisingly. The tower complex included a zoo, circus, aquarium and stunning French Renaissance-style ballroom, not to mention that all-important view from the top of the tower. This picture postcard was purchased at the tower and is stamped, 'Posted from the top of Blackpool Tower. 518 feet high.'

Opposite above: Blackpool's North Shore had not one but three impressive promenades. With miles of promenade, gardens and entertainment, Blackpool's seafront was considered one of the most resplendent in Britain. This picture was taken by the colonnades, 1914.

Opposite below: The stepped terracing of Princess Parade, 1922.

Left: Like hundreds of thousands of children before her, this child gazes down from the top of the tower on the world of fun and entertainment below. This particular child is a very young Paula Yates, who in her adult life was to find fame as a TV presenter. (Copyright The Jess Yates Estate)

Below: View from the tower looking northwards towards the Metropole Hotel, 1918.

BLACKPOOL FROM THE TOP OF THE TOWER.

The Savoy Hotel opened in 1915 and originally had 300 rooms. It advertised as offering garage space too – something altogether new in its day.

The Imperial Hydro Hotel pictured in 1934. As with many of the other great seafront hotels, it has a colourful history. In the First World War, the army commandeered the hotel and it served as a military hospital for injured officers. It is still one of the most prestigious hotels in Blackpool and several prime ministers, including Sir Winston Churchill, are past patrons of the hotel. During conference season in 1963, the behind-the-scenes battle for the leadership of the Conservative Party was fought within its walls.

The Norbreck Hydro Hotel, seen here in 1957. At the time the hotel boasted it could offer swimming, tennis, golf, bowls, dancing, and beauty therapies, not to mention foam, brine and steam baths – the complete holiday under one very large roof! The Norbreck had been commandeered during the Second World War and was not handed back by the government until 1951. Ten miles of carpet were used in its refurbishment before the hotel's reopening in 1952.

Strollers walk along the cliffs at Norbreck, *c.* 1927. To the rear of the picture is the Norbreck Hydro Hotel.

Dating back to the 1850s, Uncle Tom's Cabin was a lively entertainment house perched precariously on the sea cliffs. Over time the buildings were lost and new structures erected by the owners. It became a venue renowned throughout the district for its dancing and other entertainments. This particular view shows Uncle Tom's Cabin in 1890.

Horse-drawn carriages outside Uncle Tom's Cabin, 1907. A year later the buildings were demolished and rebuilt on a new site on Queen's Promenade.

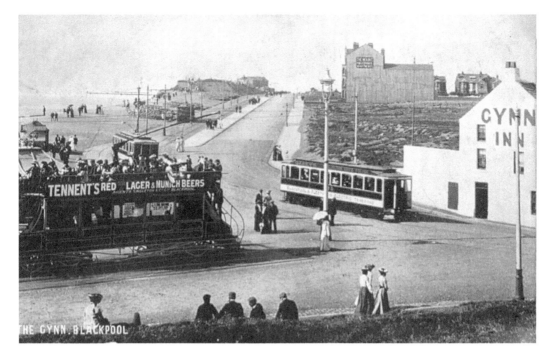

Scene around the Gynn Inn in 1905. By this time, the sea cliffs had been reduced in height to produce infill for the promenade extension. The famous old Gynn Inn itself closed in 1921 and was later demolished to make way for a new road and tramway extension.

The Gynn Inn, c. 1909. This famous old inn was a popular landmark until its closure in 1921. Many old tales still persist about the Gynn Inn. In 1833 it was reputed that a Scottish sloop was saved from being wrecked by candlelight emanating from the inn.

With its reputation for bracing sea air and leisure pursuits, Blackpool was an obvious place of rest for convalescents. This superb convalescent home was established on the North Shore for mine workers affected by breathing difficulties and HRH the Prince of Wales, later to become the Duke of Windsor, officially opened it in 1927. This picture dates from 1931.

This small white obelisk stood for a short time in Princess Parade to act as the town's temporary memorial to the fallen of the First World War. It was unveiled in 1919.

Left: Blackpool's war memorial was first unveiled on Armistice Day in 1923 and offered a highly prominent expression of the town's grief at the loss of so many men on the battlefields of Flanders and France. Erected at a cost of £17,000, the obelisk is reputed to have been funded from the profits of the Tramways Department.

Below: A view of Princess Parade and the cenotaph, 1922. The parade replaced the earlier iron walkway and was officially opened in 1912 by Princess Louise, Duchess of Argyll.

PRINCESS PARADE & CENOTAPH, BLACKPOOL

two

Around
Blackpool

Bustling street scenes of people, trams or horses and carts are evident in many Victorian and Edwardian images taken around Blackpool. This picture of Talbot Square was taken in 1925 and shows just how thronged with people the area could become.

Centre stage in this 1907 image of Talbot Square is Blackpool Town Hall. It was built between 1895 and 1900 and its magnificent spire was arguably its most striking feature until 1966, when it was declared unsafe and sadly removed.

TOWN HALL, TALBOT SQUARE, BLACKPOOL.   Copyright.

Above: Blackpool Town Hall, *c.* 1908. Blackpool was granted its charter of incorporation in 1876 and became a County Borough in 1904 – a status it retained until local government reorganisation in 1974.

Below: This 1923 picture shows the Central Public Library & Art Gallery. Worthy of note from this period image are the horse-drawn carriages waiting outside. The library was built with funds donated by the Scottish philanthropist Andrew Carnegie and was officially opened by Lord Shuttleworth in 1911. The gallery was built with money from the wealthy benefactors John and Cuthbert Grundy and houses a permanent collection of British paintings.

Abingdon Street Market is still a thriving marketplace but it has an altogether different origin. From 1862 until 1893 the market site housed Blackpool's first police station.

To the left in this picture of Abingdon Street is Blackpool's main post office. The fine Portland stone-faced building was built in 1910, replacing the headquarters that had stood previously on Coronation Street. The impressive portico of the Winter Gardens can be seen in this street scene from 1921.

A view of Layton Cemetery showing the Church of England chapel, 1956. Blackpool's principal cemetery was established in 1871 and is renowned for being the burial ground of the great and good from Blackpool's past. Amongst the notables buried here are two surviving soldiers from the Charge of the Light Brigade and Dick Barlow, the one-time England test cricketer.

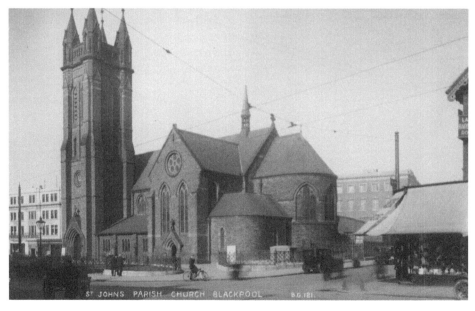

Undoubtedly one of the finest churches in the district, Blackpool Parish church (St John's) is one of the most commanding features of the town centre. The church was founded in 1821 and rebuilt in 1878, incorporating within its fabric the organ, bells and other features from the original church. St John's was blacked out during the Second World War and continued services as normal. On Easter Sunday in 1941 and on the national day of prayer the week earlier, over 4,000 people worshipped at the church.

Church of the Sacred Heart, Blackpool.

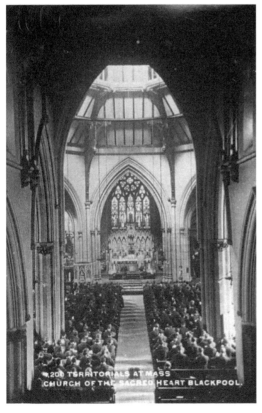

Above: The church of the Sacred Heart is the principal Catholic church in Blackpool. It was founded in 1857 and previous to that time services were held at the Railway Hotel. The church is actually brick-built but cleverly disguised with stone facing, as designed by a twenty-year-old architect. An octagonal extension to the building was added in 1894. This view of the church dates from 1925.

Left: Beneath lofty columns, this picture reveals the territorials at mass, sometime in the 1930s. There are many fine features within the church including its superb organ, the pipes of which came from the former Waterloo Cinema organ.

Above: An interior view of St Stephen-on-the-Cliffs. This Anglo-Catholic church on Holmfield Road was consecrated in 1927. One of the most striking features of the church is the Actors' Chapel. This is dedicated to the theatrical fraternity that settled locally. Stained glass windows and the chapel altar depict entertainers and there is also a marble floor memorial to Jenny Tiller of the Tiller Girls.

Right: One local church not to have drawn much praise for its appearance was Christ Church on Abingdon Street. Indeed, the great architectural historian Sir Nicholas Pevsner wrote of its appearance, 'everything is done to avoid beauty.' The church was built in 1866 and demolished in 1982. This view of the church is from 1906.

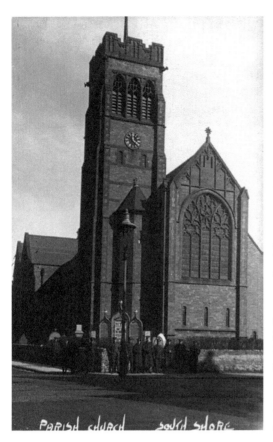

Parish Church South Shore

Left: The rather grand Holy Trinity parish church on Dean Street was opened in 1895 on the site of the earlier church built here sixty years before. The grade II listed church contains many beautiful stained-glass windows, including a number taken from the Rawcliffe Street Methodist church before it was demolished. The Lady Chapel on the south of the chancel is dedicated to the memory of Revered Burgess, the curate of the parish who was killed in a motor crash in 1911.

Below: The church of Christ, Scientist on the corner of Whitegate Drive and Gloucester Avenue. It was founded in 1929 and designed by Halstead Best, one of the best-known architects of the district in the 1930s.

Opposite above: An aerial view of the town revealing the gridiron pattern of streets in north Blackpool. The Metropole Hotel and Blackpool North railway station can easily be picked out in this picture. Owing to the emerging fashion of car ownership, restrictions were soon placed on the behaviour of careless motorists. Traffic wardens were first appointed to plod the streets in 1938.

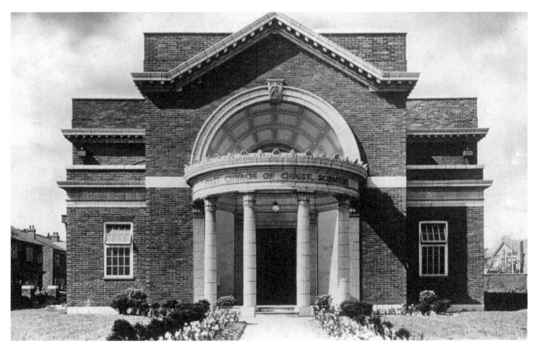

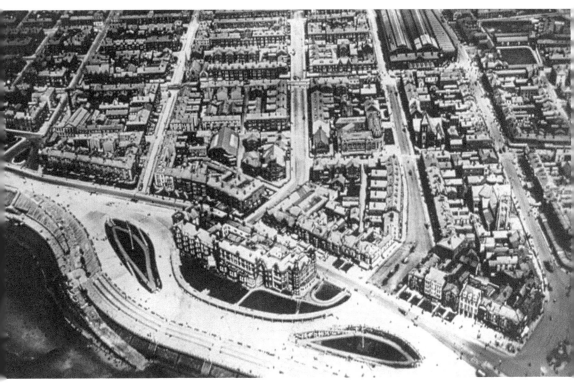

Below: Church Street, *c.* 1905. This view looks east from the old Liberal Club. The house seen to the centre is 'Cedar Villas', and behind it the roof of the Hippodrome. The entrance to the Winter Gardens is seen to the right of the picture.

BLACKPOOL GREAT WHEEL

Above: Brisk gossipy shops and a superb mix of goods were the hallmark of Victoria Street and it continues to be in the centre of the town's retail hub. This street scene dates from 1910, shortly after Blackpool's Aviation Week, which would explain the overprinting of a plane in the postcard.

Left: More than a century before the London Eye was conceived, Blackpool's Great Wheel dominated the town-centre skyline. The 220ft structure opened in 1896 in the hope of being a serious rival to the tower. It was capable of carrying thirty passengers in each of its thirty carriages. The journey itself lasted all of thirty minutes and gave a bird's-eye view of the town.

Opposite above: A unique view from Adelaide Street of both the tower and the Great Wheel. The 1,000ft structure was demolished in 1928.

Opposite below: Ribble Road, *c.* 1905. The road is still a busy residential street but, more than a century later, the motorcar now holds sway on the streets of the town.

Wheel and Tower from Adelaide St. Blackpool

A view of Withnell Road at the junction of Bond Street, 1905. This street close to the Pleasure Beach is now crowded with bed and breakfast houses.

Raikes Road Blackpool

The view along Raikes Road, as seen from the junction of Raikes Parade, 1924. The building to the right is the Blackpool Secondary School. Raikes Road was later renamed 'Church Street'.

Another view of the Blackpool Secondary School: its foundation stone was laid in 1904 on the very day that Blackpool became a County Borough. The school was built on land which was previously occupied by the entrance to Raikes Hall.

Blackpool High School, 1911.

The view along Woodfield Road in 1914. This South Shore road is now full of guesthouses serving visitors to the nearby Pleasure Beach.

Guesthouses in Albert Road, 1917.

HORNBY. ROAD.   BLACKPOOL

Above: You can almost feel the humdrum nature of everyday life in this pre-First World War picture of Hornby Road. These were the days when everybody knew his or her neighbours and a close-knit spirit existed in communities.

Below: A pleasant view of where else but Pleasant Street. There was a tenfold increase in the town's population during the thirty-year period leading up to 1900. The North Shore road was one of hundreds of streets to be built to meet the increasing need for new homes in the burgeoning resort town.

Boarding establishments abounded in Victorian and Edwardian Blackpool. Roads off the promenade were bordered with lodging houses. Pictured here is Trafalgar Road around 1906.

Church Street, 1908. Wide pavements and canvas awnings were attractive features in many Edwardian streets.

A rare picture of the old People's Castle on the North Shore in the 1930s. The castle is now a casino and partly disguised by the large extension added to the existing building.

A picture postcard showing the Symbol Biscuit Factory at Devonshire Road, 1953. The town has quite a heritage of biscuit production with handmade Brandy Snaps and other biscuits being baked here since the 1920s. Blackpool also has the lesser-known distinction of being the town that produced the first airtight packaged biscuits!

Height: 210 Ft.
Internal } *8 Ft. 6"*
Diameter }

It is often overlooked but the huge influx of holidaymakers to Blackpool generated large amounts of rubbish and its disposal was an important task for the Corporation. One of the tallest features of the town was the 210ft chimney of the town's refuse destruction works.

three

That's
Entertainment

When it opened in 1863 Blackpool's North Pier was heralded as the finest marine pier in the country. It quickly became known for the quality of its seafront entertainment, particularly high-class orchestral music. Some of the greatest vocal and instrumental artists of the day performed at the Pier Pavilion. This view of the pier dates from 1915.

A crowd of music lovers seated by the bandstand on the North Pier, c. 1920.

The 'Royal Roumanian Sextette': one of the many guest artists from abroad who toured England and performed at the North Pier, 1908.

The Royal Follies who performed on the Central Pier, 1935.

Minstrel troupes and other performing pierrots have been appearing along Blackpool's seafront since the nineteenth century. These costumed entertainers are the Rainbow Pierrots, who performed sketches of comedy, song and dance at the South Pier in 1953. Visitors to Blackpool at this time were certainly not stuck for choice; across the town fourteen live shows were on offer.

Above: Visitors to Blackpool's three piers have invariably been able to make their own entertainment. This picture postcard from 1910 shows the then new-fangled craze of roller-skating on the Central Pier.

Opposite above: The Palace was one of Blackpool's most prestigious venues for entertainment. Originally opened in 1899 and then known as 'The Alhambra', this superb pleasure palace housed a theatre, ballroom, circus, cafés and most other attractions. It was demolished in 1962 to make way for the Lewis's store.

Opposite below: Blackpool's superb Odeon opened in 1939 and, with 3,088 seats, was the second largest Odeon cinema ever built. This view shows the front of the Art Deco building in September 1946 when Jess Yates paid tribute to the favourite stars of Blackpool's victory season. The Odeon became a triple-screen cinema in 1975 and has since changed to Funny Girls. (Copyright The Jess Yates Estate)

THE PALACE, BLACKPOOL.

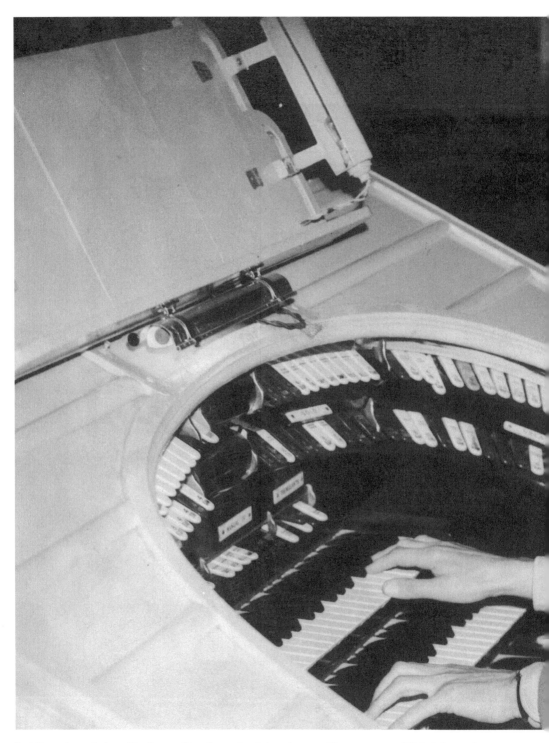

Jess Yates pictured alongside George Formby at the Odeon in 1946. Yates was one of Britain's top cinema organists and later developed a remarkable career with the BBC – as a designer, TV presenter, writer, producer and director. His hit TV shows include *Picture Parade* and *Stars on Sunday*. George Formby

was himself no stranger to entertaining the crowds at Blackpool. The little chap with the ukulele even switched on the Illuminations in 1953. (Courtesy The Jess Yates Estate)

Winter Gardens, Blackpool.

ntrance to Winter Gardens, Blackpool

Above: A grand entrance for a mighty grand building: view inside the entrance to the Winter Gardens, 1914.

Right: The Victoria Street entrance to the Winter Gardens, 1905. The imposing façade was built in 1896 and is one aspect of the complex that is still present today.

Opposite above: Along with the tower, the Winter Gardens were another expression of Blackpool's grandeur as a place for entertainment and merriment. Opened in 1878, the ornate pleasure palace was billed with the advertising slogan, 'sixpence to see and hear all.' This print from 1890 shows the building as it looked at that time. Finally housed within the complex were the Empress Ballroom, Opera House, Palm Café, Pavilion, Renaissance Restaurant, Spanish Hall, Baronial Hall, open-air skating rink, and the Olympia.

Opposite below: A view of the Winter Gardens' Church Street entrance seen from Abingdon Street, 1904. Visitors here entered the building under its mighty 120ft-high dome and were met with statues, fountains and an array of accompanying foliage.

THE ENTRANCE WINTER GARDENS, BLACKPOOL.

Left: A picture postcard view of the Indian Lounge, 1905. The room acted as a reception area for visitors to the ballroom but also, during the season, instrumental concerts were given here. There was a time when dance teas were served for patrons intending to enjoy the early-evening organ recital.

Below: The magnificent Empress Ballroom was completed in 1896. With a floor space of 12,500 square foot, it became one of the largest ballrooms in the world and its ornate appearance was meant to rival the wonderful ballroom at the tower.

EMPRESS BALLROOM WINTER GARDENS, BLACKPOOL. Photo By M.& R. SAIDMAN. 5001

Above: The Della Rosa Band pictured in 1905. These Neapolitan singers and musicians appeared at the Winter Gardens in 1900 and made many popular returns in the years that followed.

Right: Blackpool Tower, *c.* 1923. The tower is an iconic landmark for entertainment. Its stunning ballroom has played host to the very best of dance and even hosted the BBC TV series *Strictly Come Dancing* with Bruce Forsyth and Tess Daly.

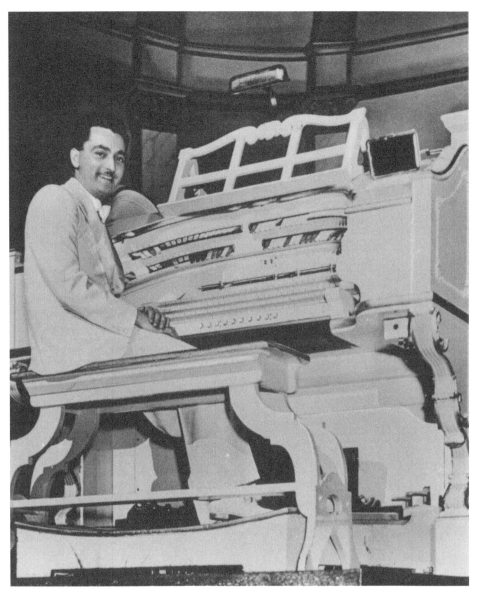

An incalculable number of celebrities have graced the stages of Blackpool, yet one of the best-loved entertainers was Reginald Dixon. He was resident organist at the Tower Ballroom's Wurlitzer for almost forty years until his retirement in 1969. His mighty Wurlitzer organ was installed at the Tower Ballroom in 1935.

Opposite above: As well as dancing, cabaret and other forms of entertainment have also been welcomed at the tower. Madame Pauline Rivers established children's ballet in 1902 and played a hand in many shows down the years. 'Hurry Along to Pleasureland' with the Allied Revue Girls was one of her shows, pictured here in 1918.

Opposite below: Another Pauline Rivers production in the 1922 season. This is the set of 'My Lady's Work Basket'.

Left: Seaside variety in the Edwardian era had a distinct over-indulgence in novel entertainers. Not surprisingly Londy, the 7ft 6in bohemian giantess, was an attraction when performing along with her 2ft 7in duo partner.

Below: And in a similar vein of quirkiness, John Lester's Midgets Miniature Minuet were also providing shows at the tower.

Above: The clowns and entertainers of Blackpool's Tower Circus assemble for this postcard pose. The world-famous Tower Circus began in 1894 and has been enthralling crowds for more than a century. It was not the first circus to have entertained visitors to Blackpool: the town was visited by touring circuses in the 1860s and a tented circus was established in the garden of Raikes Hall in 1871.

Right: The Grand Theatre opened in 1894 and became the property of the Tower Co. in 1909. From the 1920s it became a noted venue for plays and musicals prior to London West End openings. Noel Coward premiered two of his plays here in the 1940s and for a while, the theatre flirted with cinema before emerging into the 1950s and a glittering decade of star-studded summer seasons, even in spite of the growth of television. In 1981 the Grand Theatre hosted a royal variety performance, during a rare move out of the capital.

Many celebrities have trodden the boards of Blackpool's famous Grand Theatre including Arthur Askey, the diminutive comic actor who was a treasure chest of catchphrases. In the 1950s and '60s, Askey enjoyed many summer seasons performing at the Grand.

Not all of Blackpool's entertainment has been produced for a seated live audience; some has also been broadcast into millions of homes. Seen here is the set of the BBC television show *Music for Pleasure*, broadcast from the Jubilee Theatre on Sheppard Street. (Copyright The Jess Yates Estate)

four

Memorable
Moments

They didn't quite know it at the time but the laying of the foundation stone for Blackpool's new tower was an event of national significance, giving rise to one of Britain's most famous and enduringly popular attractions. Countless people have entered the building and climbed the 518ft tower since Sir Matthew White Ridley laid its foundation stone in 1891.

Between 1909 and 1911 the promenade was widened to accommodate a burgeoning number of visitors and to enhance sea defences. Blackpool Corporation's construction work required hundreds of thousands of tons of sand to be moved and relocated. To undertake this work, five small steam engines were put to work along the developing promenade. This picture from 1911 shows two of these engines and the short-lived railway track that once ran along the promenade.

Whoops! During promenade construction, one of the so-called 'sand express' carriages accidentally overturns by the Metropole Hotel, 1911.

In May 1912 Blackpool rejoiced at a royal visit from HRH Princess Louise, accompanied by her husband, the Duke of Argyll. Queen Victoria's daughter was in town to officially open the new widened promenade. This rare picture postcard shows the Princess's carriage making its way though the town en route to the promenade.

THE PRINCESS LOUISE
THE DUKE OF ARGYLL
AND W.W. ASHLEY Esq. M.P.
AT BLACKPOOL

Many thousands of people lined the streets of Blackpool and flags and bunting flew to welcome
Princess Louise and the Duke of Argyll. In this crowned view the royal couple, accompanied
by W.W. Ashley MP, pass through Talbot Square in 1912. To coincide with the royal visit, the
promenade was illuminated for the very first time.

Royal occasions have been celebrated with exuberant enthusiasm in Blackpool and this was
especially true just over twelve months later for the visit of King George V. In July 1913 the whole
of Blackpool went crazy for the arrival of the monarch; streets were gaily decorated with bunting
and streamers and more than half the town's population watched the king's procession through
the town. This particular view shows pavements lined with spectators in advance of the king's
imminent arrival from a tour of other Lancashire towns.

King George V and Queen Mary prepare to leave the Town Hall, 1913.

The royal car is almost ready to depart from the steps of the Town Hall. The queen is already seated in the car, whilst the king is seen approaching the vehicle, 1913. The royal visit to Blackpool was a brief stop – lasting in total all of half an hour!

The scene on the Princess Parade on the occasion of the royal visit of King George V and Queen Mary in July 1913. A band can be seen playing in the centre of the picture, drawing little attention from the resting spectators.

During the First World War, an exact replica of the trenches on the frontline at Loos in Flanders was painstakingly recreated on a field off Latham Road. It was used by the army and later opened to the public to provide an impression of the unparalleled ferocity of the fighting in the real Flanders fields. Any profits derived from public visits to the trenches were donated to the King's Lancashire Military Convalescent Home in Blackpool.

BLACKPOOL NORTH PIER
ON FIRE SEPT. 11, 1921

In September 1921 the North Pier was subject to a devastating fire that resulted in the loss of the Indian Pavilion along with all the instruments of the orchestra. On the reverse of the postcard, the sender writes, 'the fire commenced at 4.45 p.m. on Sunday and fifteen minutes later was burnt level with the pier. The fire is thought to have been caused by a thrown away lighted cigarette. No loss of life, business on pier as usual.'

The years 1923 and 1924 were marked in the calendar of Blackpool's social life. The Corporation organised carnivals in the town and the finest pomp and pageantry were on display when the carnival arrived. This view shows the procession of decorated floats at the 1923 carnival week.

During the carnival, fancy dress competitions were held and entered by people wearing caricature papier-mâché heads. The mounted police viewed in this picture were particularly well received by the crowds in 1923.

The 1924 carnival procession is shown here passing along the promenade. Gaily decorated floats, ceremonial bands and entertainers drew large crowds. Sadly, the festivities in 1924 were marred by hooliganism and the event was not repeated in later years.

A horse-drawn float passes along the promenade in the 1924 carnival procession.

Nurses pose for a picture at the King's Lancashire Military Convalescent Home, *c.* 1918. The Squires Gate hospital cared for soldiers injured in the First World War, providing a place for them to recuperate.

In September 1935 disaster came from the skies above Blackpool when two planes collided in mid-air. The collision caused an Avro aircraft to crash in Swainson Street, bursting into flames and drawing thousands of people to the crash scene. The streets around St John's church were almost impassable, such was the interest caused by the crash. The crash resulted in the death of the pilot and two passengers, one of whom was thrown from the plane and fell to her death in Leopard Grove.

Opposite above: The trades procession at Blackpool Carnival, 1938.

Opposite below: Seventeen years after the first devastating fire, North Pier history repeated itself in dramatic style in June 1938. Once again on a Sunday evening, a discarded cigarette was thought to have caused the blaze in the Indian Pavilion. Large crowds of spectators assembled along the sands and the promenade and commentators later estimated that 200,000 people watched the inferno.

Left: A hand-signed picture portrait of Alderman Walter Newman. He had the distinction of being Mayor of Blackpool during the town's 1936 diamond jubilee year.

Below: One matter always sure to make the news has been the destruction of Blackpool's famous shoreline. Over the last century, a great deal of effort has been needed to maintain defences against the sea and storm damage has repeatedly made the headlines. Shown here is some of the damage to the North Shore in the Easter storms of 1904.

NORTH PIER PAVILION, BLACKPOOL, ON FIRE.

PHOTO EVENING GAZETTE, BLACKPOOL.

This aerial view shows a column of fire sweeping hundreds of feet into the air from the blazing structure, 1938. Laurence Wight's On With the Show Company were performing at the time and lost almost all their instruments in the blaze. In a determined style befitting their name, the company managed to borrow equipment and instruments and resumed performances the next evening from the pier's Arcade Pavilion.

The Duchess of Westminster visited the Blackpool premises of Premier Coaches in 1942.

five

Beside the
Seaside

The construction of Blackpool's first pier was met with considerable merriment in the town. In fact, more than 20,000 people joined a procession to celebrate the North Pier's opening in 1863. It became – and arguably still is – one the finest marine piers in Britain for entertainment. Its best-known attraction was the magnificent Indian Pavilion that authentically replicated the Temple of Binderabund in India.

Strollers seen along the pier, with one of Britain's best-known waterfronts in the background, 1904. Shown from left to right are: the Great Wheel, the Alhambra building and Blackpool Tower.

Above: Please take a seat: the amazing sight of 3,000 deck-chaired holidaymakers on the North Pier, some time in the 1930s. In its first year, half a million patrons visited the pier and many more millions have visited since.

Below: Aerial view of the seafront in 1956.

A view along the promenade frontage of the North Pier in the 1940s.

Blackpool's historic Central Pier opened in 1868. The 1,518ft structure was originally known as the South Pier until such time as the third and most southerly pier was built in 1893. The stunning structure was unpopular at first as it was located some distance from the town centre but in time, with the introduction of steamer services and amusements across its decks, the pier began drawing in crowds. This view of the Central Pier is from 1909.

This 1949 picture postcard shows how busy the area became with visitors. The building to the right in this scene is the RNLI lifeboat station opened in 1937. It housed *Sarah Ann Austin*, the lifeboat service's new motor lifeboat.

Take your partner by the hand: the crowded scene on the Central Pier as people enjoy an afternoon dance, *c.* 1908. Dancing became a feature of the pier very early in its history. A band was employed to perform for passengers returning from pleasure trips.

Opposite above: Nobody knows who first introduced donkeys to the sands but generations of children are thankful they did, 1905.

Opposite below: Regulations first introduced in 1942 control the way in which Blackpool's 200 donkeys work on the sands. Known locally as the 'donkey charter', it states that the animals are expected to have a day off work and break times on the days they do work. This image shows donkey riders on the sands in 1904. Note much of the promenade area in the background has not yet been developed.

Right: 'That's the way to do it': for many decades, Punch & Judy shows have enthralled spectators on Blackpool sands. The portrayal of this classic tragicomedy was performed by four generations of the Green family, stretching back to the 1880s. One other local puppeteer to have appeared on the sands was J.H. Moore.

Below: Spades at the ready: children enjoy building sand castles on the beach, 1922.

By gum!- it's champion at Blackpool.

Dresses are hoisted up to the knees in this period postcard image from 1911.

A rare glimpse of an oyster seller's cart on the sands, _c._ 1913. This picture was probably taken before the Corporation began licensing tradespeople and entertainers on the sands and Punch & Judy puppeteers, ventriloquists, shrimp and oyster sellers, rock sellers and ice-cream stalls all vied for trade.

Short trips aboard pleasure boats were an ever-popular attraction, *c.* 1912. For many people, the beach was the perfect place to enjoy the summer sunshine, though it was sometimes difficult to find space to sit on the sands.

ON THE SANDS IN FRONT OF TOWER, BLACKPOOL.

Another crowded beach scene, 1913. It is interesting to note the beach fashions on show in this old picture postcard; long pleated dresses and cloth caps are clearly the flavour of the day. Deckchairs were not allowed on Blackpool sands until 1914.

Located near to Uncle Tom's Cabin, the seafront boating pool was a popular attraction with children. It was even once suggested that the pool had been influential in pioneering the amusement of children's paddle boats.

Gipsy encampments on Blackpool's South Shore were established long before the development of the pleasure beach. In the 1890s the gypsies were viewed as a tourist attraction but were later moved on, as they were considered peripheral competitors to the rides being developed in the locality. This particular image shows a typical gipsy tent and caravan on the sands.

six

All at Sea

Above: Blackpool has always been associated with the sea and many of the town's first settlers were fishermen. Boats have long drawn the attention of visitors to the seafront, as in this photograph of a crown. Dating from 1896, it shows crowds of people gathered to watch the yacht leader. The boat was owned by one of Blackpool's old fishing families.

Left: The scene of swirling canvas sails on the seafront became a common sight from the turn of the century. At this time, sailing boats could be hired from the promenade and they were regulated to ensure seaworthiness and good repair, 1906.

Almost ready for the off, passengers embark on a sailing boat at one of the beach's sailing slips, 1908. From the Metropole to the Central Pier, the beach was divided into three sectors, each being licensed to a different boat-owning co-operative.

Two pleasure yachts pictured on the seafront, *c.* 1910. By the late 1940s there were six co-operatives with twenty-two sailing craft.

The development of a pier in 1863 made possible the beginnings of Blackpool's love affair with pleasure steamers and a trip from either the North or Central Pier was all part of the Blackpool experience. The paddle steamer *Bickerstaffe* came into service in 1879 and served excursionists at Blackpool for almost fifty years. Her afternoon departure was timed to coincide with the closure times of local pubs.

The great days of the Lancashire pleasure steamers are brought to life in this 1905 image of the paddle steamer, *Queen of the North*. The 590-ton ship was built in 1895 and was owned by the Blackpool Passenger Steamboat Co., offering pleasure excursions to the Isle of Man. She was later requisitioned in the First World War for use as minesweeper but was lost on active service in 1917. This 1905 picture postcard shows the *Queen of the North* with Captain Harry pictured insert.

THE "GREYHOUND."

One of the best-known early pleasure boats to operate at Blackpool was the Blackpool North Pier Co.'s coast paddler *Greyhound*. The 306-ton Clyde-built ship serviced routes to Llandudno and Douglas during the summer season and operated sailings to Liverpool on Sundays.

THE "GREYHOUND" AT BLACKPOOL.

The *Greyhound* prepares to moor alongside the North Pier in 1910. During the First World War, this paddle steamer was requisitioned for use as a minesweeper and, after returning to service in 1919, operated just four more seasons at Blackpool before being sold for use at Belfast.

Above: Wrapped up warmly, even on a summer's day in 1912. This picture shows pleasure ship excursionists aboard the paddler *Greyhound* as she prepares to sail.

Below: Full steam ahead! The steam ship *Midden* sets sail from Blackpool fully laden with pleasure trippers. The former Mersey ferry was bought by the newly formed Blackpool Pleasure Steamers Ltd in 1933 and served for five seasons before being sold to the breaker's yard in 1938.

Storm at Blackpool, Feby. 1903

Above: A howling storm at Blackpool pictured in 1903. Many ships had been wrecked on the Fylde coastline over the centuries and locals have salvaged the shoreline wreckage. In 1821 *The Fanny* was wrecked off the coast, laden with black and red flannel, and as a result for many years to come it was not uncommon to see Blackpool folk wearing 'Fanny Petticoats'. In 1861 a ship was wrecked on the South Shore laden with a cargo of flour and lard. Presumably there would have been plenty of baking that week.

Below: Crowds watch the lashing waves in 1924.

Arguably the most celebrated wreck to beach on Blackpool's foreshore was the *Foudroyant*. In 1897 Nelson's flagship broke free of her moorings between the Central and North Piers and ended her illustrious life aground on a bank by the Metropole Hotel. Thousands of anxious shoreline watchers cheered as *Foudroyant's* crew were taken to safety by a Blackpool lifeboat.

Blackpool's lifeboat service began in 1864, arising from the fact that local fishermen were risking their own lives to rescue crews. The first lifeboat was a relatively unstable ten-oared rowing boat named *Robert William*. Such was the joy at her arrival that 20,000 people attended the boat's naming ceremony. This particular antique postcard pictures the later lifeboat *Samuel Fletcher* and her crew on the sands, in around 1910.

BLACKPOOL LIFEBOAT CREW 1908.   WOLSTENHOLME. PHOTO. WELLINGTON STUDIOS BLACKPOOL.

A portrait of the lifeboat crew in 1908. The local volunteer crews have attended at some heroic rescues down the years. In one rescue, they were at sea for twenty-eight hours and at another incident in howling gales the lifeboat men crewed and brought into land a schooner that had been abandoned by her own crew.

BLACKPOOL LIFEBOAT, LEAVING THE BOATHOUSE.

The lifeboat *Samuel Fletcher* is pictured here leaving the lifeboat house on Lytham Road. Established in 1864, this was the first lifeboat station and it remained in use until a new boathouse opened by the Central Pier in 1937. The *Samuel Fletcher* was a twelve-oared boat but also carried sail. She was in service between 1896 and 1930 and in that time attended at twelve rescues, saving the lives of twenty-eight people.

In 1880 the lifeboat *Robert William* battled through one of the fiercest storms ever encountered at Blackpool to aid the crew of the stricken schooner *Bessie Jones*. The crew of the Fleetwood ship took refuge from the extremely cold conditions within the schooner's rigging. Four lives were saved that night and each member of the lifeboat crew won the RNLI Silver Medal for their bravery. Washington Hotel landlord George Barrett painted this image of the lifeboat going to the rescue of the *Bessie Jones*.

Blackpool's first motor lifeboat went into service in 1937. *Sarah Ann Austin* had a top speed of almost 7 knots and, in the event of her engine failing, also carried sails. She was officially launched by the Duke of Kent, president of the RNLI, and took part in many daring rescues over the coming years.

This view of the *Sarah Ann Austin* shows her carriage mounted on the sands in the 1950s. The lifeboat service's most active period came during the Second War World when she was launched fifteen times to search for crashed aircraft. The lifeboat crew mainly recovered wreckage but at one launch in 1944 they rescued three airmen afloat in dinghies. The *Sarah Ann Austin* remained in service until 1961, by which time she had saved thirty lives.

Including temporary lifeboats and inshore craft, the Blackpool lifeboats over the last 143 years have been called to 1,126 services. During that time, the lives of 387 people have been saved. This image shows the Blackpool lifeboat in 1907 passing through rough seas on just one of those rescues.

Fishing boats seen off Blackpool in 1907. Blackpool's first industry helped give rise to the growth of the fledgling town.

Boats have not only sailed to and from Blackpool, but the town has even sailed the seas. Since the Second World War, two Royal Navy warships have borne the town's name: the first was a Bangor-class minesweeper, launched in 1940 and later sold to the Norwegian Navy. Pictured here is the latter, HMS *Blackpool*, the Whitby-class frigate that saw service from 1957. The warship had an active service life and was loaned to the New Zealand Navy for five years prior to being used for monitoring underwater explosive tests. HMS *Blackpool* was scrapped in 1978.

seven

At Your Leisure

Recreation and sport form an important part of any town's past and that is equally true of a resort town like Blackpool. Opened in 1926, Blackpool's Stanley Park was thought of as a landscaping masterpiece, even in its day. The 274-acre parkland rivalled any of the finest parks in the country and included amongst its facilities a 100-acre golf course, cricket ground, football, tennis, bowls and an impressive array of gardens, including the wonderful centrepiece Italian gardens. This 1936 picture shows the park's floral clock.

The boating lake in Stanley Park was one of the park's best-loved leisure facilities. In the early days of the park, the former Blackpool lifeboat *Samuel Fletcher* was used as a pleasure boat on the lake. Stanley Park was placed on the national register of historic parks in 1995.

A recent view of the Italian gardens photographed during Stanley Park's £5 million restoration. In the background is the Cocker Memorial Clock built in 1927 to commemorate the life of Alderman W.H. Cocker. He was Blackpool's very first mayor, a position to which he was elected on six occasions.

Arguably Britain's best-loved and most popular amusement park, Blackpool Pleasure Beach has been drawing visitors for over a century. Founded by William George Bean in 1896, the Pleasure Beach was his attempt to create an American-style amusement park. This 1926 postcard view shows some of its best-known attractions in those early days. From left to right are: Maxim's Flying Machine, Noah's Arc, Scenic Railway and the Rainbow Pleasure Wheel.

THE HELTER SKELTER SLIDE, SOUTH SHORE, BLACKPOOL. 3243

Above: Sir Hiram Maxim's Captive Flying Machine was one of the most popular early attractions. This 1904 postcard was printed and in distribution just days after the opening of the ride and the massive crowds drawn by these whirling rides can be seen here clearly.

Left: The Helter Skelter, 1905. It is thought that this lighthouse-style Helter Skelter was likely to be the very first in the country. In the background can be seen Sir Hiram Maxim's Captive Flying Machine.

Opposite above: The roller coaster Big Dipper was built in 1923 and was for many years the key signature ride of the pleasure beach. It became a landmark for many miles around and is still in use today.

Opposite below: The 'River Caves of the World' ride opened in 1905. Fun seekers paid 3d to meander along in a boat through recreated grottos and caverns. The track to the left of this picture is the Hotchkiss Bicycle Railway that William George Bean had brought from the United States.

The Casino at the Pleasure Beach, pictured here in 1933. The building included a theatre, billiard room and restaurant and was decoratively illuminated at night. The Casino was demolished in 1937 to make way for a new, more modern style of building. However, the old structure would not go without a fight; explosives had to be used to demolish its thick concrete walls.

The new Casino building was officially opened in 1939 by Lord Stamp, president of the LMS Railway. This view of the Casino is from a 1946 postcard.

The Casino and Pleasure Beach, 1954.

An aerial view from 1923 of the South Shore's new open-air swimming baths. This stunning-looking facility was undoubtedly one of the finest pools of its kind found anywhere in the world and was even reputed to have been based on a design inspired by Rome's Coliseum.

In the first years following its 1923 opening, over one million people are said to have used the new facility. This view of swimmers is also from the 1920s.

Crowded terraces at the open-air baths often viewed swimming contests and beauty pageants. Many important events were held here, including the crowning of the Cotton Queen and Miss United Kingdom. The baths even featured in the 1934 Gracie Fields film, *Sing as We Go*. The film portrayed Fields as a Lancashire mill worker enjoying high-spirited adventures at Blackpool.

BLACKPOOL FOOTBALL CLUB

Above: Blackpool Football Club was formed back in 1887 but has its origins in other smaller local clubs stretching back even further. It joined the Football League in 1896 and finished a respectable eighth in their first season. The club had varying degrees of success until 1930 when they won the division two championship. This cigarette card shows the Blackpool team in the 1930s.

Below: The Blackpool FC team photograph from the 1956/57 season. The late 1940s and 1950s were the glory years of 'The Seasiders' – between 1948 and 1956 the club reached three FA Cup finals and were first division runners up in 1956.

Bloomfield Road – the ground of
Blackpool Football Club, 2002. The
home ground of 'The Seasiders' now
has a seating capacity of 9,000. Back in
1955, the ground hosted a club record
attendance of 38,000 for a match
against Wolverhampton Wanderers.
(Copyright Newton Ashley)

Above: The team pictured in the 1959/60 season. It still included many of the all-time Blackpool greats including Stanley Matthews, George Farm and Jimmy Armfield, who made a record 626 appearances for the club.

Left: Arguably the greatest and most renowned player ever to grace English football, Stanley Matthews joined Blackpool in 1947 and remained with the club for fourteen marvellous years. The right-winger achieved his greatest triumph in 1953 when he helped the club to a last minute FA Cup final victory over Bolton Wanderers. Football fans still refer to it as 'the Matthews final' and it remains Blackpool's most famous triumph.

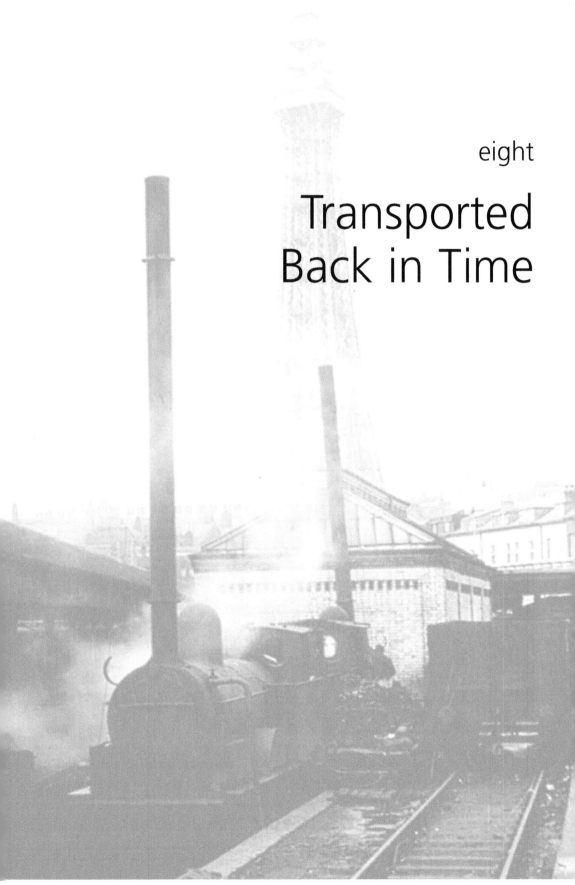

eight

Transported Back in Time

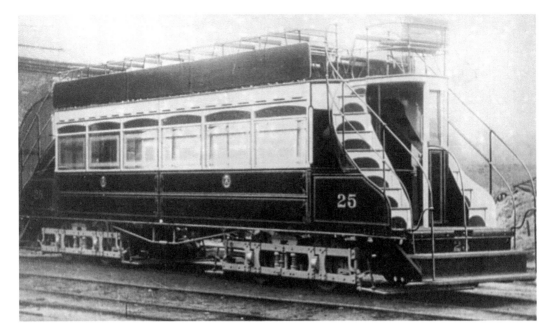

Blackpool's world-famous trams were inaugurated in 1885 and have the distinction of being Britain's first electric street tramway system. The original service operated with ten trams along a two-mile length of the esplanade but expanded greatly over the coming decades. By 1910, Blackpool's trams were carrying nine million passengers a year. This picture shows one of the original dreadnought trams that were in use before the turn of the twentieth century.

Originally the trams operated on a conduit line but in the late 1890s, the trams converted to using overhead electric cables, as can be viewed in this picture. This view shows another of the dreadnought trams at the Gynn Inn terminal, c. 1905. This tram serviced the new lines that were brought into service between Blackpool and Fleetwood in 1899.

This undated view shows the dreadnought tram number 59, en route to Central Station. This particular tram was built in 1902 and was surprisingly still in service in 1964, when it was being sponsored by and renamed *The Daily Mirror Tram*. However, for the most part these open-top double-staircase dreadnought trams disappeared from frontline service in the 1930s.

A busy street scene at Talbot Square showing people queuing for a journey on one of the new toastrack trams, *c.* 1912.

Toastrack tram number 70 entered service in 1911 and operated on the new five-mile circular tour route.

The so-called 'toastrack' trams were extremely popular with summer holidaymakers, provided of course that the weather was fine. These sixty-nine-seat open-top single-deck trams cost just 4d per journey and helped ensure the circular tour route was a good earner for the Corporation. In this view, passengers prepare to depart for a journey aboard a toastrack.

This rather solemn-looking group of trippers on the circular route pose for a photograph, *c.* 1912.

A toastrack passes along Whitegate Drive, *c.* 1913. The circular route ran from Talbot Square, passing up Clifton Street, Abingdon Street and Church Street en route to Whitegate Drive. From here it passed along Waterloo Road, Lytham Road and back along the Promenade. This particular tram was built in 1912 and scrapped in 1939.

Tram rides have always been part and parcel of the unique Blackpool experience and commitment to trams has never waned here. In the 1930s, many towns and cities were ripping out their tramlines in favour of motor buses but at Blackpool, a hundred new streamline trams were being put into service. This picture shows one of the old Blackpool & Fleetwood Tramway Co. cars passing along the promenade, 1930.

These new 'ballroom-style' trams came into service from 1934. The eight-four-seat trams were able to accommodate larger numbers of passengers and were ideal for use on the promenade. This particular tram is travelling from the Pleasure Beach to Manchester Square, c. 1938.

A tram passes by the tower building in 1952. In the 1950s, 150 trams were still in use, transporting forty-five million passengers a year on the various Blackpool routes.

Two standard Blackpool trams, 1966. The tram to the right is embellished with lamps ready for evening use on the Illuminations tour.

The so-called 'boat' was another design of open-top tram that came into service in the 1930s to replace the old toastracks. This particular tram came into service in 1935 and remained in use until 1972.

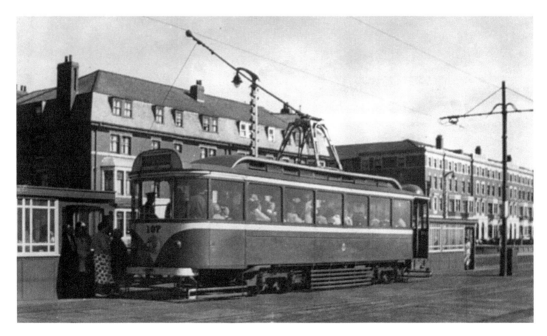

Above: A 1928 Pullman tram pictured in 1951.

Opposite above: By the 1950s, day-trippers were flocking to Blackpool on coaches and parking needed to be provided. This East Midlands Albion coach is a typical model of the time, pictured at Rigby Road coach park in 1953.

Below: Although overshadowed by the fun of journeying on one of Blackpool's famous trams, local bus services have played an essential role in the town's transport infrastructure. This picture from 1966 shows the number 5 bus on the promenade, heading north en route to the Grange estate. These were the days when conductors still took payment and helped passengers on and off the bus.

Another 1966 view, this time showing a Leyland Burlingham bus heading along the promenade on route 6B.

The railway age came to Blackpool in 1846 when a branch line of the Preston & Wyre Railway was constructed to a new railway station at Talbot Road. It spurred on the development of tourism in the fledgling resort town and people began arriving in ever increasing numbers, particularly from the industrial heartlands of the North West. This impressive building was the second, later station building on the site, opened in 1898. This picture postcard view of Talbot Road Station is from 1911.

This image shows the main entrance to the station in 1912. The Station Hotel can be seen to the left of this picture and on the right is the imposing canopied entrance to the main hall. The station was later renamed Blackpool North and despite subsequent demolition and rebuilding down the decades, this name still remains in use today.

A stationary Lancashire & Yorkshire Railway's steam engine seen at Blackpool North Station, 1951.

SUNDAY, 4th OCTOBER, 1953

SEASIDE EXCURSION

TO

BLACKPOOL

(NORTH)

FROM	TIMES OF DEPARTURE	RETURN FARES (Third Class)	ARRIVAL TIMES ON RETURN
	a.m.	s. d.	a.m.
†NOTTINGHAM (Midland)	9 30	} 14/9	2 53
BEESTON	9 39		2 44
ATTENBOROUGH	9 44		2 38
LONG EATON	9 53		2 31
STAPLEFORD & S.	10 0	14/3	2 25
TROWELL	10 6		2 18
ILKESTON JUNCTION	10 11		2 13
LANGLEY MILL	10 20	13/3	2 5
ALFRETON & S.N.	10 34	} 12/9	1 51
WESTHOUSES & B.	10 39		1 45
DOE HILL	10 44	12/6	1 39
†CLAY CROSS	10 55	12/-	1 27
	p.m.		p.m.
BLACKPOOL (North) arrive	2 30	...	depart 10 0

FOR DETAILS OF LATE 'BUSES AT NOTTINGHAM AND CLAY CROSS

—see overleaf.

Travel in Rail Comfort

Blackpool came to throng with railway excursionists and at no time more so than during the Illuminations. This British Railway's bill from 1953 details one of the special seaside excursions being made from Nottingham to Blackpool North.

The great steam age is revived in this old picture postcard from 1905. The train shown is Lancashire & Yorkshire Railway's Blackpool Express. In its earlier days, the line was a single track and services were not renowned for either speed or punctuality. The impetus for a second line to Blackpool grew with some momentum, resulting in 1863 with the opening of Blackpool & Lytham Railway, a line passing through the south of the town to a new central station.

Central Station, c. 1907. When it opened in 1863 the station caused an upsurge of interest in Blackpool and opened the way for the mass market of day-trippers to Blackpool. In the early 1860s alone, the number of rail passengers travelling to Blackpool doubled to 285,000 every year and kept rising for many decades to come.

What better backdrop is there to a railway platform than the towering sight of Blackpool Tower? This 1956 picture shows an out-of-service locomotive.

Above: Two end-to-end engines at the same location in 1949.

Below: The Jubilee-class steam locomotive *Irresistible* at Central Station, *c.* 1957. The service was an all-station stop to Manchester. The awe of whistles and cascading steam gripped generations of children and many local people still have vivid memories of steam trains at Blackpool.

Above: The crowded scene of carriages stationary at Blackpool Central Station in the early 1900s. There were fourteen platforms, some of which were especially for excursionists. At peak times in the morning these platforms were thronged with disembarking passengers and fuelled lively competition outside from hoteliers anxious for their passing trade. At peak departure times there might only have been a matter of minutes between trains.

Left: A selection of bell-punched tickets for train services to and from Blackpool in the heyday of rail travel. By the 1950s, visitors were increasingly likely to use the family car to reach the town and this downturn in fortunes for the railways led to the closure of Central Station in 1964.

Opposite above: Blackpool has played an important role in the early history of aviation and images of planes over the town are seen in many early picture postcards. In October 1909, the town hosted what was to be the second ever aviation show in Britain, the first having started three days earlier at Doncaster. Many leading British and foreign aviators took part in the event at Squires Gate.

Below: All eyes on the sands and promenade would have looked skyways when the loud hum of a biplane passed overhead. Over 50,000 people attended the first day of the aviation show at Squires Gate, proving that these primitive flying machines were an immense draw to the public. One of the highlights of this week in 1909 was when Hubert Latham, flying his *Antoinette* monoplane, reached speeds of 40mph in high winds – something that had previously been thought impossible.

FLYING AT BLACKPOOL.

FLYING AT BLACKPOOL.

A biplane approaches for a bumpy landing in 1909.

A view of Hubert Latham flying his *Antoinette* monoplane at the first Blackpool flying week, 1909. One of the most famous early aviators, Latham was the first man to attempt to fly the English Channel but after two failed attempts lost out on the prize to Louis Blériot. He later set a world distance record for flying and also achieved a world record plane speed of 48mph. Latham was killed in the Congo in 1912.

This souvenir postcard from the first aviation show at Blackpool imposes an image of Henry Farman's fragile-looking biplane over the promenade. Another Frenchman to have made headlines that week, Farman set a new record distance for a flight of 47 miles in one and half hours.

A second flying carnival was held at Blackpool in 1910 and history was made that week when mail was carried by plane for the very first time anywhere in the world. One of the leading exhibitors at the second event was French aviator Claude Grahame-White. This image shows the Frenchman's biplane leaving his Squires Gate hangar amidst a crowd of admiring onlookers. During that week Grahame-White flew around the tower and on to the Isle of Man. In 1910 he also won the distinction of becoming the first man to land a plane at Southport and was narrowly beaten to the £10,000 *Daily Mail* prize for flying from Manchester to London.

Flying at Blackpool.

After the First World War, the Avro Aviation Co. were operating scheduled flights to Blackpool. In 1919 the first ever scheduled passenger flights out of Manchester took place between a Manchester airfield

and Blackpool's South Shore. Avro biplanes were also used to provide pleasure flights from the sands and were an immensely popular sight for spectators, as is evident in this view, *c.* 1920.

Other local titles published by The History Press

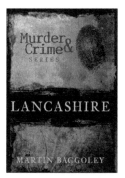

Murder & Crime in Lancashire
MARTIN BAGGOLEY

This selection of true crimes from across Lancashire are as diverse as the locations in which they were committed, including mass murder and suicide in Salford, a vicious assault over a wager in Liverpool and a sweetheart shot to death in Southport. Contemporary illustrations complement the text to provide a shocking and compelling account of the darker side of the Red Rose County.

978 07524 4358 4

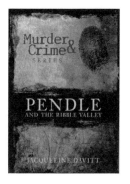

Murder & Crime in Pendle and the Ribble Valley
JACQUELINE DAVITT

This fascinating book contains tales of thwarted rivals and wicked soldiers, desperate mothers and disreputable women. With more than 50 illustrations, this chilling catalogue of murderous misdeeds is bound to captivate anyone interested in the criminal history of the area.

978 07524 4495 6

From a Gin Palace to a King's Palace Music Hall in Preston
DAVID JOHN HINDLE

'Raise the tabs, for I proudly present the most popular, scintillating and devastatingly dependable music hall, packed with song and dance, novelty acts, special guest turns, and side-splitting banter for your sincere unmitigated enjoyment…' With a foreword by *Coronation Street*'s Betty Driver and a preface by Preston North End legend Sir Tom Finney, this is an essential guide to the history of music hall in Preston and across the entire country.

978 07524 4453 6

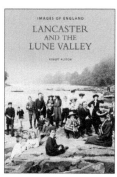

Lancaster and the Lune Valley
DR D.J. ALSTON

This fascinating collection of more than 180 old photographs traces some of the many ways in which Lancaster has changed over the last century. A valuable historical record of life in the ancient city, this book depicts almost every aspect of daily life and will reawaken nostalgic memories for many.

978 07524 3007 2

If you are interested in purchasing other books published by The History Press, or in case you have difficulty finding any of our books in your local bookshop, you can also place orders directly through our website
www.thehistorypress.co.uk

This book is dedicated to Doreen & Harry.

Frontispiece: Aerial view of Blackpool in the 1930s when seven million people a year were flocking to the town – almost double the number of people visiting the resort twenty years earlier. What had started as a centre for cotton workers widened its appeal to become Britain's best-known and best-loved tourist resort.

First published in 2007 by Tempus Publishing

Reprinted in 2010 by
The History Press
The Mill, Brimscombe Port,
Stroud, Gloucestershire, GL5 2QG
www.thehistorypress.co.uk

Reprinted in 2011

British Library Cataloguing in Publication Data.
A catalogue record for this book is available from the British Library.

ISBN 978 0 7524 4494 9

Typesetting and origination by Tempus Publishing
Printed and bound in Great Britain